ENERGY IN, ENERGY OUT:
FOOD AS FUEL

Crabtree Publishing Company
www.crabtreebooks.com

Series Development and Packaging: John Burstein, Slim Goodbody Corp.
Senior Script Development: Phoebe Backler
Managing Editor: Valerie J. Weber
Designer and Illustrator: Ben McGinnis
Graphic Design Agency: Adventure Advertising
Instructional Designer: Alan Backler, Ph. D.
Content Consultant: Betty Hubbard, Ed. D., Certified Health Education Specialist
Project Editor: Reagan Miller

Library and Archives Canada Cataloguing in Publication

Burstein, John.
    Energy in, energy out : food as fuel / Slim Goodbody.

(Slim Goodbody's lighten up!)
ISBN 978-0-7787-3914-2 (bound).--ISBN 978-0-7787-3932-6 (pbk.)

    1. Body weight--Regulation--Juvenile literature. 2. Energy metabolism--Juvenile literature. 3. Nutrition--Juvenile literature.
I. Title. II. Series: Goodbody, Slim. Slim Goodbody's lighten up!
QP171.G66 2008   j612.3'9
C2008-900724-7

Library of Congress Cataloging-in-Publication Data

Burstein, John.
  Energy in, energy out : food as fuel / John Burstein.
    p. cm. -- (Slim Goodbody's lighten up!)
  Includes index.
  ISBN-13: 978-0-7787-3914-2 (rlb)
  ISBN-10: 0-7787-3914-7 (rlb)
  ISBN-13: 978-0-7787-3932-6 (pb)
  ISBN-10: 0-7787-3932-5 (pb)
  1. Body weight--Regulation--Juvenile literature. 2. Energy metabolism--Juvenile literature. 3. Nutrition--Juvenile literature. I. Title. II. Series.

  QP171.B872 2008
  612.3'9--dc22
                        2008003593

Crabtree Publishing Company

www.crabtreebooks.com   1-800-387-7650

Published in Canada
Crabtree Publishing
616 Welland Ave.
St. Catharines, Ontario
L2M 5V6

Published in the United States
Crabtree Publishing
PMB16A
350 Fifth Ave., Suite 3308
New York, NY 10118

Published in the United Kingdom
Crabtree Publishing
White Cross Mills
High Town, Lancaster
LA1 4XS

Published in Australia
Crabtree Publishing
386 Mt. Alexander Rd.
Ascot Vale (Melbourne)
VIC 3032

"Slim Goodbody" and "Lighten Up with Slim Goodbody" are registered trademarks of the Slim Goodbody Corp.

Printed in the U.S.A.

TABLE OF CONTENTS

Slim Goodbody's
LIGHTEN UP
SERIES

HELLO THERE. I'M SLIM GOODBODY,

and my greatest goal in life is to help young people across the planet become healthy and active. After all, one in three kids in the United States is overweight. Without changing their eating and exercise habits, many of these young people will become overweight adults. They risk many possible health problems like **high blood pressure** or **diabetes**.

Today, I would like to introduce you to my friend Shantelle. She's a high school student and has always dreamed of becoming a model. Now is her big chance! Shantelle may get a job at Beautiful Balance Modeling Agency. Join her as she learns about modeling, healthy eating, exercise, and beauty.

A Dream May Come True

Ever since I was a little girl, I've wanted to be a model. I love trying on new clothes and pretending to walk down the runway. At the beginning of the summer, I went to the Beautiful Balance Modeling Agency. When they invited me to take their modeling classes over the summer, I was thrilled. At the end of the classes, the agency will decide if I have what it takes to be a model!

I came to the agency on Monday, eager to start my classes along with ten other teens. I was so excited and tried to look as glamorous as I could.

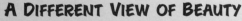

A Different View of Beauty

Lucille, one of the agents at Beautiful Balance, welcomed us to the agency and asked us to introduce ourselves. I tried to remember everyone's name as they said them—Rachel, Jerome, Tawnya, Jorge, Luke, Douglas, Abby, Maria, Lamont, and Kaitlin.

Lucille had big green eyes and a dazzling smile. "I am delighted to welcome you to Beautiful Balance. We think about beauty differently here compared to most other modeling agencies. We believe that being beautiful means being healthy.

"If you look in magazines today, you'll see men and women who are so skinny that they look like bare bones wearing makeup. Those models are considered **underweight**. That means that they don't eat enough to be sure their bodies get the **nutrients** that they need to stay healthy. If teen models are underweight, they may not reach their proper height, and may find it hard to fight off infections.

Of course, you've probably also seen kids in your neighborhood who are overweight or **obese**. These are serious problems, too. Many health problems can develop from being overweight or obese. Overweight kids may find playing sports or even walking difficult. They have a higher chance of growing up to be unhealthy, overweight adults, too. One of the reasons that overweight people have health problems is that they often eat foods that are high in fat and **calories**. Junk food, like candy bars and potato chips, are low in important nutrients."

A Different Way to Achieve Beauty

Lucille continued, "Here at Beautiful Balance, we are going to teach you how to take care of your bodies by eating well and exercising. If you follow our fitness and **nutrition** advice, you'll feel great, have more energy, and look beautiful!"

I couldn't believe what I was hearing—a modeling agency that believed that the key to beauty was being healthy! I always thought that models had to be really thin to look good. Before I could question Lucille, she was introducing a new teacher.

"Meet Louis, our nutrition expert at Beautiful Balance. He's going to teach you how to keep your body at a healthy weight," said Lucille.

WHAT IS A HEALTHY WEIGHT?

Louis led us into a classroom. Rachel raised her hand as we sat down. "Louis, I have a problem with what Lucille said earlier. She made it sound like you have to be a certain weight to be healthy and beautiful," she said.

"You know," Louis responded, "everyone has their own idea of what a healthy weight is. Some people think that they need to look like a super thin supermodel to be beautiful. Others like to have round curves and a little more padding on their bodies. The truth is that a healthy weight depends on your age, **gender**, body build, and activity level. A great way to find out if you are at a healthy weight is to use this chart," said Louis, pointing to a chart on the wall. "It will help you measure your **Body Mass Index**, or BMI."

What's that?" asked Luke.

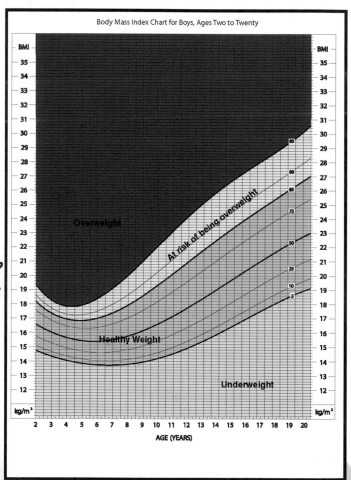

Body Mass Index Chart for Boys, Ages Two to Twenty

A HEALTHY MEASURE

"Your Body Mass Index is a measurement of your body fat based on your height and weight. This measurement shows if you are in a healthy weight range for your height. You can see if there's a healthy balance between your fat tissue and lean tissue, like muscle, bones, and organs. People your age use this equation to find out your BMI," explained Louis.

Weight (in pounds) / stature (in inches) / stature (in inches) x 703 = BMI

"First, write down your height in inches and your weight in pounds. Jerome here is 6 feet, or 72 inches, tall. He weighs 190 pounds," said Louis, pointing to one of the older teens.

"Then, I divide Jerome's weight by his height. 180 / 72 = 2.5

I take that number and divide it by his height again. 2.5 / 72 = .0347

Then, I multiply that number by 703 to find out Jerome's Body Mass Index. .0347 x 703 = 24

Finally, I look on the BMI chart. I look to see where the lines for his age and Body Mass Index number meet. Does he fall in the *underweight, healthy weight, at risk of being overweight,* or *overweight* category?"

I raised my hand. "He is in the healthy weight category."

"You're right, Shantelle. Now everyone, go ahead and use this same equation and chart to figure out your own BMI," said Louis. "You can also use the website at http://apps.nccd.cdc.gov/dnpabmi/Calculator.aspx

BMI: MAYBE A REASON TO CHANGE
We all got to work. As we finished, Louis said, "Remember, it can be difficult to determine the Body Mass Index for kids. If your BMI is in the overweight category, it may be because you have recently had a **growth spurt**. It can also mean that you need to get more exercise and eat a healthier diet, however."

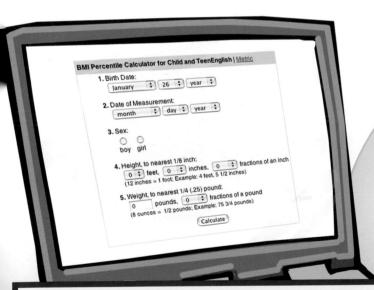

http://apps.nccd.cdc.gov/dnpabmi/Calculator.aspx

Slim Goodbody Says: You can figure out your own Body Mass Index by using this equation and chart, too. There's a version of the BMI charts for boys and girls on page 31. Ask your teacher, parents, or doctor if you need help calculating your BMI.

7

ENERGY IN, ENERGY OUT: AN IDEAL BALANCE

"To keep your body at a healthy weight, you have to balance the energy coming in with the energy going out," explained Louis. "Does anyone know how our bodies take in energy?"

I raised my hand and said, "By eating food."

"That's right, Shantelle. Energy from food is measured in calories. If you look on the back of a food container, you'll find the nutrition label. At the top of the label, you can see how many calories are in each serving. Now, how do you burn energy?"

Jorge answered, "By exercising."

THE ROLE OF CALORIES

"If you exercise often, you can burn 20 to 30 percent of the calories that you eat. But your body also needs calories to breathe, digest, stay at a normal temperature, and keep your heart beating. The number of calories that you burn for these basic functions is called your **basal metabolic rate**. Kids also need calories to grow and to produce new tissue, like bone, muscle, and blood."

"But if you don't burn all of the calories that you eat, your body stores them as fat, right?" asked Kaitlin.

"That is very true, Kaitlin. Your body needs some fat to protect your internal organs. Young people also store fat to grow later in life. But you still need to make sure that you're balancing the calories that you eat with the calories that you burn. Here is a little chart that will help you see how many calories you should eat depending on the amount of exercise that you get each day," explained Louis.

	Age	Sedentary Lifestyle	Moderately Active Lifestyle	Active Lifestyle
Girls	9-13	1,600 calories	1,600-2,000 calories	1,800-2,200 calories
Girls	14-18	1,800 calories	2,000 calories	2,400 calories
Boys	9-13	1,800 calories	1,800-2,200 calories	2,000-2,600 calories
Boys	14-18	2,200 calories	2,400-2,800 calories	2,800-3,200 calories

"If you are **sedentary**, it means that you don't exercise and only burn the calories that your body needs to do normal, day-to-day activities. These activities would include going to school or doing your homework. If you are moderately active, you get some exercise, like walking at a moderate pace for 1.5 to 3 miles (2.4 to 4.8 kilometers) a day. Active people get more exercise, like walking 3 to 4 miles (4.8 to 6.4 km) a day at a quick pace," said Louis.

"So if I exercise a lot, I can eat more and tone my muscles," suggested Jerome.

"Exactly," said Louis. "Here at Beautiful Balance, we encourage all of our models to choose an active lifestyle. Good work, everyone. It's time for lunch."

Energy IN and Energy OUT

The same amount of energy IN and energy OUT over time = **weight stays the same**

More energy IN than OUT over time = **weight gain**

More energy OUT than IN over time = **weight loss**

Slim Goodbody Says: It isn't always easy to find the right balance of the energy that you take in and the energy that you burn. Keep this in mind when you are choosing what to eat and how much to exercise.

ENERGY IN: FOOD CHOICES

As our group walked over to the lunchroom, I felt my stomach rumble. I was hungry, but I wanted to remember what Louis had taught us about calories. I wanted to find something that was healthy and that would fill me up.

I turned to Abby, one of the girls in our group. "What are you going to have for lunch?" I asked.

"I don't know. I'm really hungry, though," Abby said.

"Me too. I want to make sure that I get enough nutrients, but I don't want to eat too many calories," I told her.

"I know. We'll just have to see what they have in the lunchroom. My mom always tells me to follow the *Go, Slow, Whoa* approach to eating," said Abby.

"What's that?" I asked.

"It's just a simple tool that helps me remember to eat well. *Go* foods are low in fat, calories, and sugar and have a lot of nutrients in them."

"OK, can you give me some examples of *Go* foods?" I asked.

"Fruits, vegetables, whole-grain bread, and skinless chicken are all *Go* foods," Abby explained.

"*Slow* food has more fat, calories, and sugar. Sports drinks, white bread, and low-fat microwave popcorn are *Slow* foods. I try not to eat them very often because they are not as good for me. It's funny, but I actually feel slow when I eat them," Abby continued.

"And what are *Whoa* foods?" I asked.

"*Whoa* foods are all the kinds of foods that have tons of fat, calories, and sugar in them," said Abby.

"You mean like doughnuts and French fries?" I asked.

"Yeah, and chicken nuggets, too. I only have them once in a while," said Abby. As we talked, we arrived at the buffet.

"OK. We want *Go* foods, not *Slow* and *Whoa* foods," I laughed. I chose steamed green beans and a grilled chicken sandwich on a whole-wheat bun.

"I guess I'll have an apple for dessert instead of chocolate cake," I said.

"I am going to have water instead of soda," said Abby. "Come on, let's go talk with our new classmates at that table."

11

ENERGY IN: PORTION SIZE

After lunch, we returned to the classroom. Lucille began, "I hope you all had a good lunch. It's important that you get enough food and nutrients. Otherwise, you won't be able to focus in class, and you'll get tired easily. You also need the right nutrients to make your hair shine, skin clear, and your muscles toned. Just like Louis taught you, you don't want to eat too much or too little."

HOW MUCH IS ENOUGH?

Douglas raised his hand. "That makes sense, but I'm still having a hard time knowing how much food my body needs."

"You can use a few tools to decide how much to eat," explained Lucille. "When you're at home, check out the nutrition label on the food container. Look at the top of the label to find the serving size of that food. A different number of servings are recommended for each food group. For example, both boys and girls should get 6 ounces (170g) of grains each day. A serving of bread is one slice, which weighs about 1 ounce (28g). Try to eat the serving size and recommended number of servings. Track your food for a few days, and see if you usually eat too much or too little from each food group."

Douglas raised his hand again. "But what if I'm not at home? What if I'm out at a restaurant?"

Nutrition Facts

Serving Size 1 Slice (25g / 0.9oz)
Servings Per Container 18

Amount Per Serving

Calories 70   Calories from Fat 10

	% Daily Value*
Total Fat 1g	2%
Saturated Fat 0g	0%
Trans Fat 0g	
Polyunsaturated Fat 0.5g	
Monounsaturated Fat 0g	
Cholesterol 0mg	0%
Sodium 90mg	4%
Total Carbohydrate 12g	4%
Dietary Fiber 2g	8%
Sugars 1g	
Protein 2g	

Vitamin A	0%	•	Vitamin C	0%
Calcium	2%	•	Iron	4%

Percent Daily Values are based on a 2,000 calorie diet. Your daily values may be higher or lower depending on your calorie needs:
Calories: 2,000   2,500

EXPANDING PORTIONS

Lucille nodded her head. "That's harder. Portions are getting bigger and bigger these days. A cheeseburger at a restaurant today has twice the number of calories in it as a cheeseburger served at restaurants twenty years ago. Bagels and muffins are also twice as big as they were twenty years ago. They also have more than twice as many calories in them. Sodas are more than three times the size they used to be with almost four times the calories!"

"And the more we eat these big portions, the more we think that they are a normal size. We start thinking that we should always eat that much," said Tawnya.

"Exactly. But when you eat smaller portions, you will have a much easier time keeping a balance between the energy that your body takes in and the energy that it burns," said Lucille.

Cookies

20 Years Ago — Today

Muffins

20 Years Ago — Today

Cheeseburgers

20 Years Ago — Today

French Fries

20 Years Ago — Today

Turkey Sandwiches

20 Years Ago — Today

Slim Goodbody Says: Here are some tips for cutting back on portion size:

- At home, portions should be no larger than an adult's fist.
- Order a medium pizza instead of a large. Everyone gets the same number of slices as before; they're just smaller.
- Use a smaller plate than your normal dinner plate. A small portion on a small plate won't look skimpy.
- Use tall, narrow glasses instead of short, wide glasses for unhealthy drinks. You will drink less.

ENERGY OUT: PHYSICAL ACTIVITY

The next day, we returned to the agency for our fitness class. Mike, the fitness trainer, met our group in the workout room.

"Greetings, future models!" Mike said. "My job is to teach you all about how to get fit. Physical activity is not only fun, it's an important part of keeping your body healthy. It helps you stay at a healthy weight, and strengthens your muscles, bones, and joints. Not only that, but being active can help you sleep better, have more energy, and improve your mood. I'm always in a better mood after I exercise."

"People your age should get about an hour of exercise every day," he continued. "So go ahead and find yourself a treadmill or stationary bike."

We all spread out and found a spot. Abby and I chose two bikes next to each other. After twenty minutes of pedaling, I was sweating and breathing hard.

"I don't think I can do this for much longer," I said to Abby. "Am I going to lose my chance at modeling if I stop?" I didn't want to disappoint Mike, but I felt dizzy and wobbly. I saw Mike coming over to us. He looked concerned.

START SLOWLY, BUILD GRADUALLY

"Are you OK, Shantelle? Why don't you both take a break and get some water? You're making a great effort, but you need to pace yourself. The best way to get fit is to start slow and build up your pace and the length of your workout." He smiled and gave me a pat on the shoulder.

"I just don't want to lose my chance to be a model," I said with a worried voice.

EXERCISE ONE HOUR EVERY DAY!

"We're trying to teach you how to live a healthy life. That's a lot more important than modeling," explained Mike. "Remember, good health is the best form of beauty. Once you get your water and your strength returns, you can walk at a moderate pace on the treadmill."

"Thanks, Mike," I said.

EXERCISE EVERY DAY

After we were finished exercising and cooling down, Mike gathered us together again.

"Great job, everyone. This summer, I am going to help all of you get into shape. But I need your help too. When you get home in the afternoon, make sure that you set aside an hour for exercise. You can play a volleyball game with friends, go for a bike ride, or walk around your neighborhood. It doesn't matter what kind of exercise you do, as long as you do it regularly."

Slim Goodbody Says: The number of calories that you burn while you exercise depends on your age, weight, and gender. It also depends on how hard you work out and for how long. This chart offers a general estimate of the number of calories that you will burn while exercising.

Activity	Calories Burned in 30 Minutes
Biking	95
Running	360
In-line skating	192
Sitting and doing homework	36
Swimming	237
Walking	150

NOT MUCH ENERGY OUT: SCREEN TIME

Before we left the workout room, Mike brought us together again. "I also want to let you know how important it is to limit the amount of time that you spend watching TV, playing video games, and sitting at the computer," said Mike. "Kids these days spend way too much time in front of a screen. In fact, on average, children between the ages of eight and eighteen spend six hours a day in front of TVs, computers, and video games! Six hours every day!" said Mike, shaking his head. "I don't know about all of you, but after I watch a lot of television, I feel lazy. I just don't want to go outside and be active."

"I think it's harder to eat well when I watch TV. I always want ice cream and potato chips while I watch my favorite shows," Maria said.

GET OFF THE COMPUTER

Mike nodded. "You're not alone. Studies have shown that people often eat when they are in front of a screen. Since people don't usually exercise while they watch TV, their energy in and energy out balance is way off," said Mike. "So what can you do instead of watching TV?"

"Go in-line skating," suggested Luke.

"Play baseball with friends," offered Tawnya.

"I like to exercise when I watch TV," said Jorge. "My brother and I compete to see who can do the most jumping jacks or push-ups during commercials."

"That's clever! Sometimes our lives are so busy that we have to be creative about finding time to exercise," said Mike. "But nothing can beat getting outdoors and being active. Next time, turn off that TV and go outside with your brother. Have a race, play football, or go for a bike ride. As long as your muscles are being stretched and strengthened and your heart is pumping, it doesn't matter what kind of exercise you do. Just turn off that TV!"

TURN IT OFF!

Slim's STAGGERING STATISTICS

Almost 70 percent of children ages eight to eighteen in the United States have a TV in their bedroom. On average, kids with TVs in their rooms watch 1½ hours more TV every day than kids without TVs in their rooms.

ENERGY IMBALANCE: BEING OVERWEIGHT

A few weeks later, I was feeling great. I had been exercising every day and using Abby's *Go, Slow,* and *Whoa* eating plan. I already felt stronger and healthier, and my hair and skin looked better than ever. It was fun to learn about walking on a runway and posing for photo shoots, but I was realizing that being healthy really was the best way to feel beautiful.

That afternoon, my mom drove me to my doctor's office for an appointment. I told Dr. Rose all about my new modeling classes.

"I feel so good. Why doesn't everyone get in shape?" I asked her. "There are so many kids at my school who are overweight."

A HEAVY FAMILY HISTORY

Dr. Rose nodded, "Well, there are a number of reasons that some people are heavier than others. First of all, being overweight can run in a family. If your parents and grandparents are overweight, there is an increased chance that you will be, too. Of course, that's only part of the answer. Imagine children growing up in a household where they never learn to exercise regularly or how to eat a healthy, balanced diet. They will also have a much higher chance of being overweight. As you've found out, it takes work and knowledge to stay healthy and fit," said Dr. Rose.

"That's true, but once you get used to exercising and eating well, it doesn't take nearly as much effort," I said.

"I agree. It's also very important. There are many health problems that go along with being overweight, including diabetes, high blood pressure, and high **cholesterol. Asthma** and sleep problems may be related to obesity, as well. Kids who are overweight are more likely grow up to be obese adults."

"What can overweight kids do to get healthy?" I asked.

DIET FADS

"Well, they can do exactly what you're doing. They can eat well and exercise regularly. Unfortunately, many overweight people try to fix their problems overnight by signing up for diet programs that promise fast results. Some people drink special diet formulas or skip meals altogether. Those methods of losing weight are very unhealthy. To lose weight in a healthful way, you should only lose 1 to 1½ pounds (0.4 to 0.7 kg) per week. If you lose weight by eating well and exercising, you'll have a much easier time staying at a healthy weight," explained Dr. Rose.

ENERGY IMBALANCE: EATING DISORDERS

"At school, I've heard some kids who seem to think only about losing weight. That doesn't seem healthy either," I shared.

"That's very true, Shantelle. Both boys and girls from all ethnic and cultural groups can suffer from serious **eating disorders**. They become overly concerned about their weight and the way that their bodies look, or their body image. These problems can begin very early in life, even as young as age eight," said Dr. Rose.

"That is so sad," I exclaimed.

FEAR OF FAT

"It's a terrible problem," agreed Dr. Rose. "I have some patients who suffer from **anorexia nervosa**. With this condition, they eat very little because they fear becoming overweight."

"I had a classmate who was anorexic. It was awful. She was so skinny, but she always talked about how fat she was. Her hair even started falling out. She was a great athlete, but she quit all of her sports teams and stopped hanging out with her friends.

Her parents finally brought her to the hospital to get help," I told her.

"I'm sorry to hear that, Shantelle. You know, some people also suffer from an eating disorder that's known as **bulimia**. They eat a large amount of food in a short amount of time. Afterward, they force themselves to vomit or take laxatives to quickly get rid of the food. Their bodies don't have a chance to absorb the food's calories and nutrients.

GETTING HELP

"If you think that a friend has an eating disorder, you should encourage him or her to get help. If he or she refuses, you should ask an adult that you trust for help," Dr. Rose advised me.

"Girls are generally the ones who suffer from anorexia and bulimia, but boys can have body image troubles, too," she continued. "There's a lot of pressure on boys to be muscular today. Some boys become so anxious about being too small and skinny that they suffer from a disorder called **muscle dysphoria**. These boys often lift weights for long hours, obsess over what they eat, and sometimes even take **steroids** to bulk up. If you have a friend who is extremely self-conscious about his body, you should encourage him to seek help, as well."

"It seems like such a big problem," I told her. "After all, if people don't eat, they won't get enough nutrients to keep their bodies healthy."

"That's right. If people with eating disorders don't get help from a doctor, they can suffer from long-term health problems. The most serious cases can even end in death," explained Dr. Rose.

"Wow. I guess that's why I like the Beautiful Balance Modeling Agency so much. They teach us that we have to be healthy to be beautiful. I really believe it. The healthier I get, the better I look," I said.

21

A Big Decision

A few weeks later, we were asked to prepare a presentation on what we had learned about health, fitness, and modeling. At the end of the week, a panel of judges would choose the top five models from our group. Their reward for all their hard work? Appearing in a photo shoot for a new line of teens' clothing.

I found Abby on the verge of tears. "Shantelle, I'm so nervous. I don't think I'm going to make the cut. I want to be a model so badly, but I'm afraid I didn't lose enough weight this summer."

"What are you talking about, Abby? You've been working as hard as the rest of us. You deserve to be a model as much as anyone in this group," I told her.

"I think that I'm going to stop eating for the rest of the week. That way, I'll look thinner when I go in front of the panel," Abby said.

"Wait a second, Abby!" I said firmly. "Remember what everyone at Beautiful Balance says—to be beautiful, you have to be healthy. Skipping meals is never a good idea. It can lead to serious problems if you do it often. You have to make healthy decisions to be healthy."

22

STEPS FOR HEALTHY CHOICES

"My dad taught me a strategy to help me make healthy choices," I continued. "First, you *identify your choices*. Next, you *evaluate each choice*, and think about the consequences of each one. Then, you *identify the healthiest decision and take action*, and finally, you *evaluate your decision*."

Abby took a deep breath. "I know you're right. OK, so my choices are to eat healthy food and exercise or to skip meals for the rest of the week."

"Right. Now evaluate your choices," I encouraged her.

"If I stop eating, I'll feel terrible, and I won't be getting the nutrients that my body needs. If I eat healthy food and exercise, though, I'll have the energy that I need. I can show that judges' panel what I am really made of!"

"That's more like it, Abby! So what are you going to do?" I asked hopefully.

"I'm going to be active and eat nutritious foods. That's a lot more important than being a model anyway!" said Abby, wiping the tears from her cheeks.

"At the end of the week, you can decide if you made the right decision," I said.

"Thanks, Shantelle. You really helped me out," said Abby, giving me a hug.

Slim Goodbody Says: Now it's your turn. Use Shantelle's decision-making strategy to make healthy decisions in your own life. Maybe you can decide to turn off the TV and get some exercise? Or what about eating an apple instead of a candy bar? Just remember the five simple steps:
- Identify your choices
- Evaluate each choice. What are the consequences of each choice?
- Identify the healthiest decision
- Take action
- Evaluate your decision

At first, you will have to concentrate on following this strategy, but soon, you will do it naturally.

23

A GOAL FOR MYSELF

On the day that we would go in front of the judges, Abby and I decided to walk to the agency together. We caught up with Lamont, one of the boys from our group.

"Hey, Lamont, are you nervous about today?" I asked.

"A little," Lamont admitted. "Do you guys think that you're going to make the cut?"

"I don't know," said Abby.

"My goal is to give a great presentation in front of the panel. I can't control if the judges pick me or not, but I can make sure that I do my best. Do you guys have any goals?" asked Lamont.

"What do you mean?" I asked.

A HOW-TO GUIDE

"My dad helped me make some goals last night. He told me to *set a realistic goal and write it down.* Then, I should *list the steps to reach the goal.* We talked about how I could *get help and support from others* while I try to achieve my goal. After that, I need to *evaluate my progress,* and then, I decide how to *reward myself* if I reach my goal," explained Lamont.

"My goal is to continue to exercise and eat

well whether I get to be a model or not," I said. "To reach my goal, I'm going to write down a fitness plan for myself to make sure that I get some exercise every day. I will also use the *Go, Slow,* and *Whoa* tool to make sure that I eat healthy foods."

"What about support from your family and friends?" asked Abby.

A Team Approach

"I always have more fun exercising with friends," I told her. "It's also easier to stick with an exercise program if you do it with a friend. If you'd like to go on a bike ride with me a couple of days a week, that would be great. I can also ask my parents to make sure that they buy healthy foods at the grocery store. That way, I won't be as tempted to eat junk food."

"How will you evaluate your progress?" asked Lamont.

"I guess at the end of each week, I can decide if I followed my fitness plan and ate healthy foods," I said.

"And how will you reward yourself if you did?" Abby asked.

"I guess I should make healthy choices about my rewards, too, so that I don't undo all of my hard work. I know if I reach my goal in one month, I'll buy a new exercise outfit!"

Slim Goodbody Says: Now it's your turn to make a fitness goal. Setting healthy goals is a great way to get in shape and to follow a healthier diet. Remember the five basic goal-setting steps:

• Set a realistic goal and write it down
• List the steps to reach the goal
• Get help and support from others
• Evaluate your progress
• Reward yourself

My Big Moment

When we arrived at the Beautiful Balance Agency, we went to the dressing room. All of the other girls in our group were putting on their outfits and styling their hair. My stomach was twisted in knots, but I forced myself to get ready. This was my chance to show the judges that I was ready to be a model.

One by one, Lucille called each of us to the judging room. Finally, she smiled at me. "OK, Shantelle, you're up."

"Thanks for everything, Lucille," I said. Remembering to hold my head high and my shoulders back, I walked confidently into the room.

"Welcome, Shantelle. You can begin your presentation now," said one of the judges. I took a deep breath and began.

WHAT I'VE LEARNED

"This has been the best summer of my life. I've loved learning to be a model. After working with Lucille, Mike, and Louis, I'm convinced that being healthy is the best way to be beautiful. I never used to exercise. Now I ride my bike or walk for an hour almost every day. I hardly ever watch TV anymore. I've also been choosing foods that are high in nutrients and low in calories, fat, and added sugar. I'm also careful about eating healthy portions. When I go to restaurants, I even bring a plastic container along for my leftovers so I don't overeat. I feel healthier, stronger, and smarter than ever."

I continued confidently, "Yesterday, I set a goal to continue to make healthy choices whether or not I become a model. I have a lot of relatives who are overweight; many have serious health problems. I want to stay fit so that I won't have the same kinds of problems when I'm older. On the flip side, I want to make sure that I eat enough. I know boys and girls at my school who are so obsessed with being thin that they skip meals. I understand now that they need help. I hope that if I can live a healthy life, I can set an example for others to do the same. Thank you for this opportunity to learn how to be healthy and beautiful," I said with a big smile.

Slim Goodbody Says: Now it's your turn to summarize what you learned in this book about eating well and exercising. How can you make sure that you balance the energy that your body takes in with the energy that it burns? Make a poster of the healthy tips that you learned from Shantelle and her friends. Put it up in your room to remind yourself to

A SURPRISING CHANCE

The judges talked together after my presentation. I waited nervously, until finally Louis, the head judge, spoke. "Shantelle, we thought you did an excellent job at your presentation. We would like you to be in the teens' clothing photo shoot. We also want to offer you a job as Beautiful Balance's youth health **advocate**. You would be paid to work with Lucille, Mike, and our employees to teach teens about making healthy choices. Unfortunately, you won't be able to do both jobs, so you will have to choose."

I couldn't believe what I was hearing. "What's a health advocate?" I asked.

"A health advocate is someone who works to make his or her family, school, and community healthier and stronger. What you have to do is *take a healthy stand on an issue*. Then you work to *persuade others to make a healthy choice*. And most importantly, you have to be *convincing*," explained the judge. "Is there a message that you would like to spread?"

MY MESSAGE

"One thing that I have learned from this summer is the importance of turning off the TV and getting active. Now that I have done that myself, I can't believe how much more time I have to exercise, do my homework, and hang out with my friends," I said.

One of the judges asked, "How do you think that you would persuade someone to make healthy choices about watching TV?"

"Well, I could go to schools and explain to kids that watching TV not only wastes time, but it's bad for them too. I know that I used to eat junk food when I watched TV, and then

I didn't have any energy to go outside and get exercise. I could explain the health problems that can go along with spending too much time at the TV and computer and playing video games," I said.

"Do you think that you can be convincing?" asked one of the judges.

"Yes! I can tell them my own story. I can explain that once I stopped watching so much TV and started exercising and eating well, I had more energy. I also felt better about myself and looked great, too! Maybe if they hear that I did it, they'll feel like they can, too!"

28

The judge gave me some time to think about my choice. Should I model or become a health advocate? Finally, I decided. "I've made up my mind. I would be honored to be a health advocate. After all, modeling would be a great experience, but I would really like to make a difference in the lives of young people."

Later, I celebrated my decision with Abby and Lamont. They had been chosen to model the new teens' clothing. They also promised to help me spread my healthy message!

Slim Goodbody Says: Now it's your turn to become a health advocate. Help your family, friends, and community make healthier choices. What health issue do you care about? How can you persuade other people to make healthy decisions? Remember, we need people like you to help our families and communities become stronger and healthier. Good luck!

GLOSSARY

advocate A person who supports or speaks in favor of a cause or an idea

asthma A disease of the respiratory system that makes it hard to breathe and causes coughing

basal metabolic rate The number of calories that your body burns at rest to maintain normal body functions

calories Units of energy that are contained in foods and drinks. Calories are used to produce energy. Extra calories that are not used as energy may be stored as fat

cholesterol A fatty substance that is found in food products that come from animals, such as milk, eggs, and meats. Too much cholesterol in the blood can build up on the walls of arteries and reduce blood flow, increasing someone's chances of having a heart attack or stroke

diabetes A disease in which a person has too much sugar in the blood. A person with diabetes cannot produce enough insulin, the substance that the body needs to use sugar properly

eating disorders Any of several mental illnesses that causes people to negatively change their eating habits and their attitudes toward their weight

gender The sex of a person

growth spurt A sudden increase in height or weight

high blood pressure A condition that forces the heart to work too hard to pump blood

nutrients Chemical compounds (such as protein, fat, carbohydrates, vitamins, and minerals) that make up foods. The body uses these compounds to function and grow

nutrition The science that deals with foods and their effects on health

obese Describes someone with a much higher amount of body fat than lean muscle mass. The government's definition of an obese adult is someone with a Body Mass Index greater than 30

sedentary Being inactive

steroids Drugs that are often used illegally to build muscles. Steroid abuse can cause bone, heart, and liver damage and increase aggression

underweight Weighing less than normal weight for one's height

FOR MORE INFORMATION

Kids Health for Kids: Body Mass Index

www.kidshealth.org/kid/stay_healthy/weight/bmi.html
Learn more about the Body Mass Index and use a special calculator to find out which category you are in: underweight, healthy, at risk of being overweight, or overweight.

Dairy Council of California

www.dairycouncilofca.org/activities/pfp/pfp_main.htm
Use this tool to help determine if you are getting enough exercise in your daily life.

Kidnetic

www.kidnetic.com
Learn new healthy and delicious recipes, play games, and find tips on staying fit and healthy.

Kids Health for Kids: Go, Slow, and Whoa

www.kidshealth.org/kid/nutrition/food/go_slow_whoa.html
Learn more about the Go, Slow, and Whoa approach to eating, and learn which foods are best.

BOYS' BMI CHART

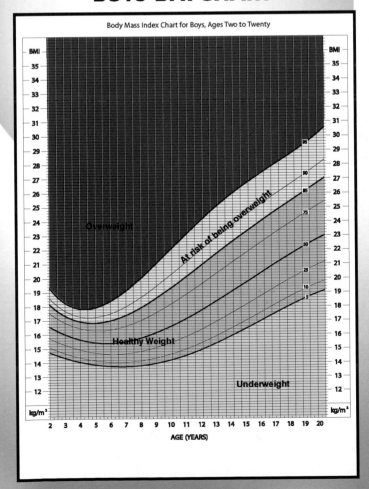

GIRLS' BMI CHART

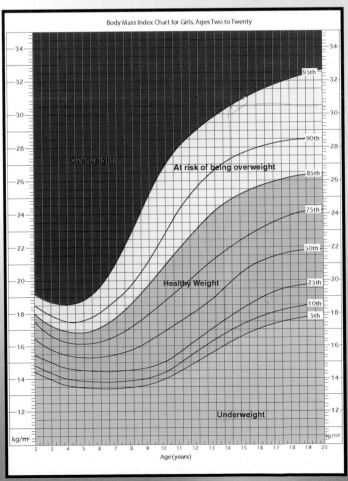

INDEX

ABOUT THE AUTHOR

John Burstein (also known as Slim Goodbody) has been entertaining and educating children for over thirty years. His programs have been broadcast on CBS, PBS, Nickelodeon, USA, and Discovery. He has won numerous awards, including the Parent's Choice Award and the President's Council's Fitness Leader Award. Currently, Mr. Burstein tours the country with his live multimedia show "Bodyology." For more information, please visit slimgoodbody.com.